EASY PIANO

2	Creator King
14	Freedom
9	Friend Of God
18	God Is Great
26	Hey Jesus Loves Me
32	I Give You My Heart
42	Let The Praises Ring
46	Open The Eyes Of My Heart
37	So Good To Me
50	Thank You, Lord
56	Trading My Sorrows
60	We Lift You Up

ISBN-13: 978-1-4234-3205-0
ISBN-10: 1-4234-3205-3

7777 W. BLUEMOUND RD. P.O. BOX 13819 MILWAUKEE, WI 53213

For all works contained herein:
Unauthorized copying, arranging, recording or public performance is an infringement of copyright.
Infringers are liable under the law.

Visit Hal Leonard Online at
www.halleonard.com

CREATOR KING

Words and Music by
MARY MacLEAN

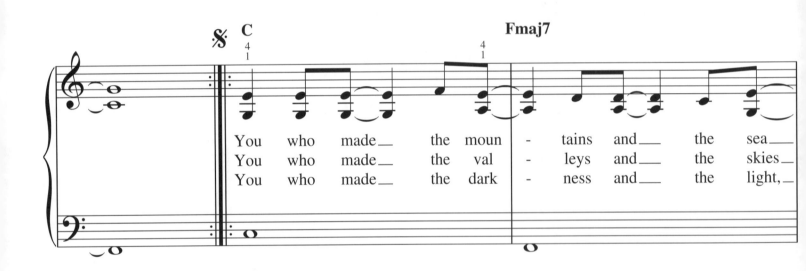
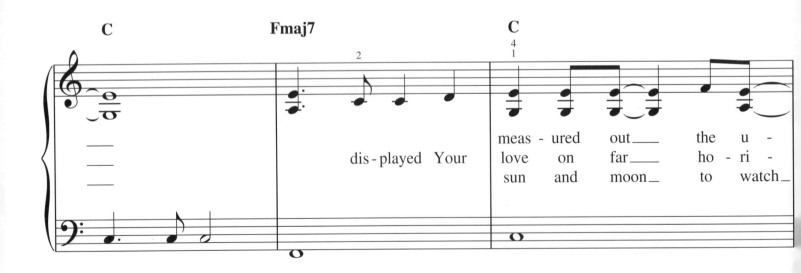

© 2003 Vertical Worship Songs/ASCAP
c/o Integrity Media, Inc., 1000 Cody Road, Mobile, AL 36695
All Rights Reserved   International Copyright Secured   Used by Permission

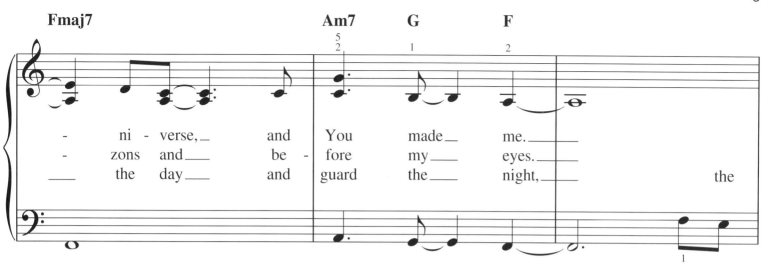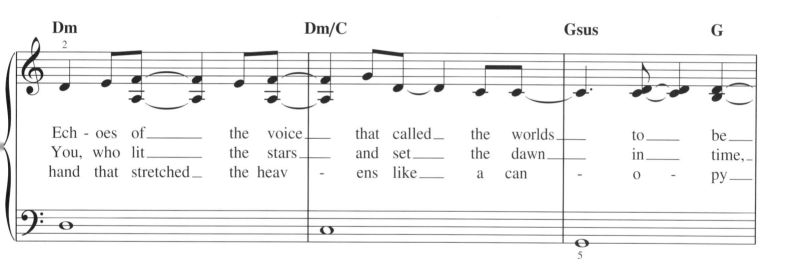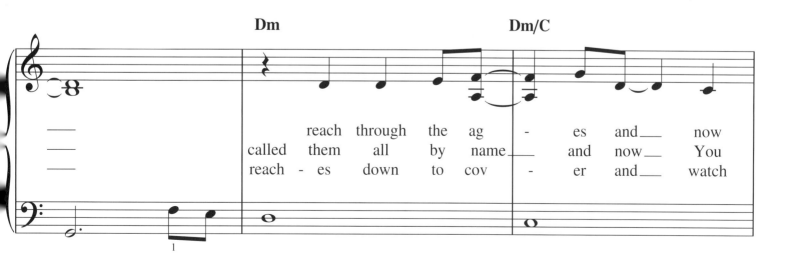

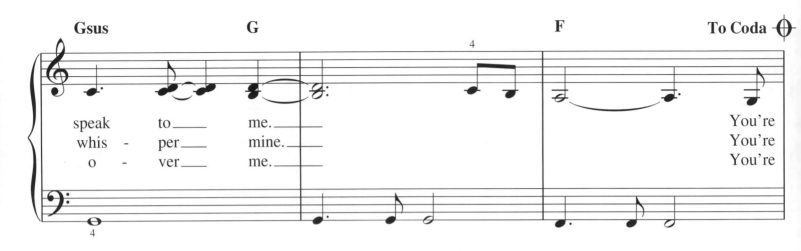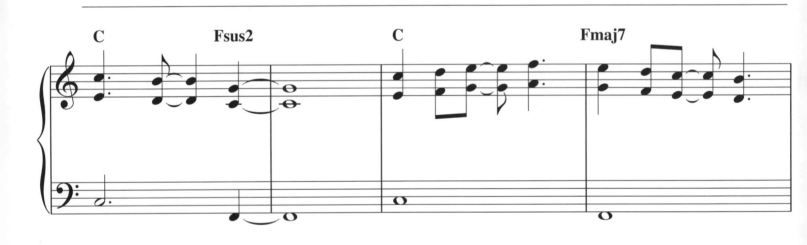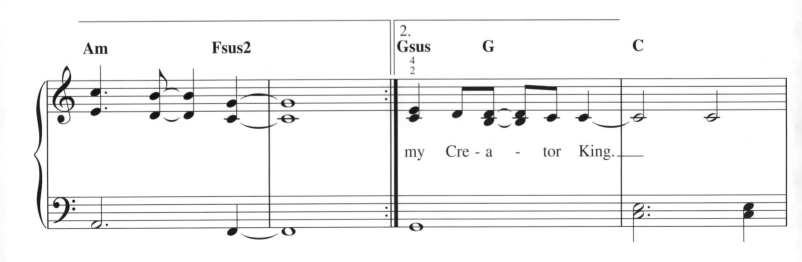

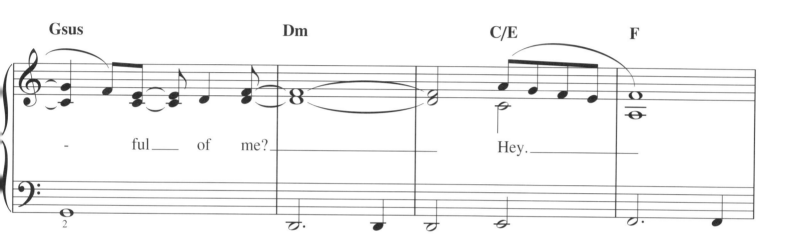

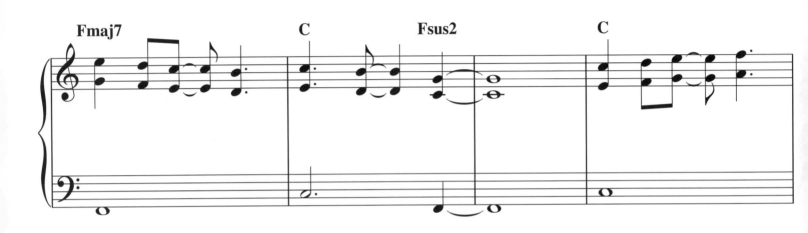

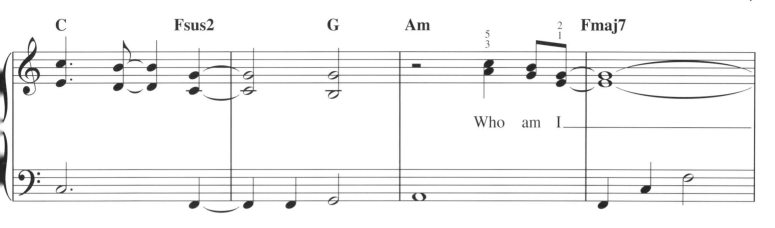

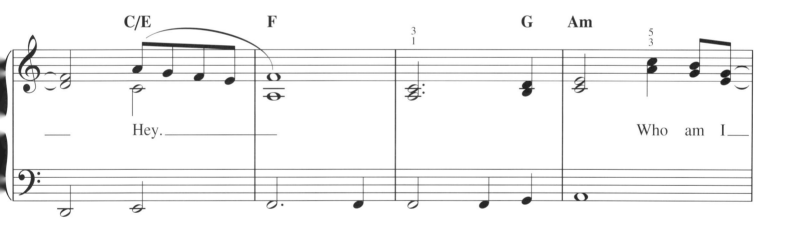

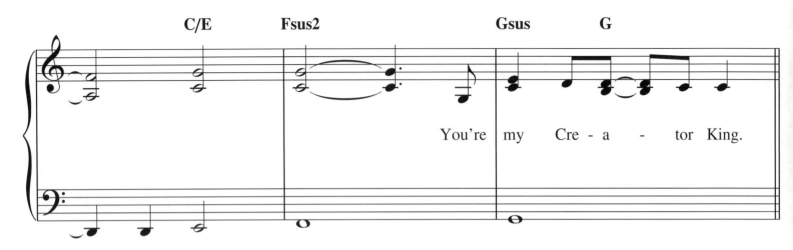

FRIEND OF GOD

Words and Music by MICHAEL GUNGOR
and ISRAEL HOUGHTON

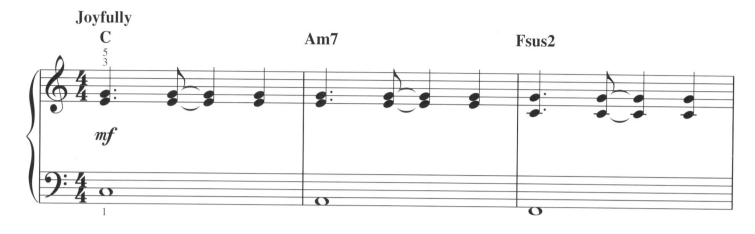

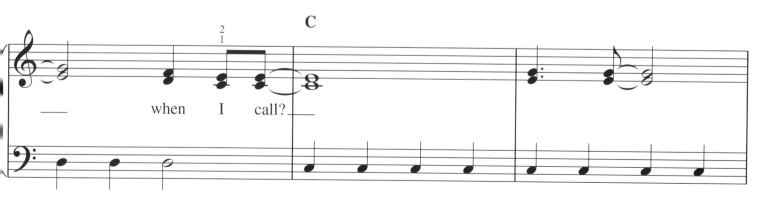

© 2003 Integrity's Praise! Music/BMI and Vertical Worship Songs/ASCAP
c/o Integrity Media, Inc., 1000 Cody Road, Mobile, AL 36695
All Rights Reserved   International Copyright Secured   Used by Permission

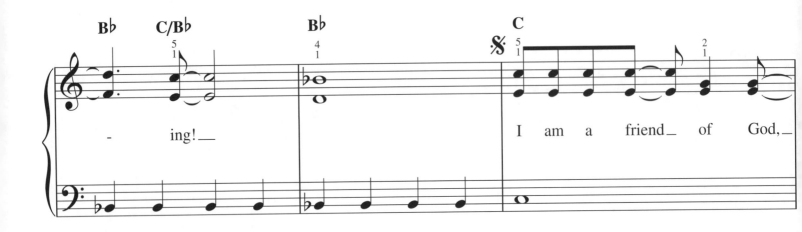

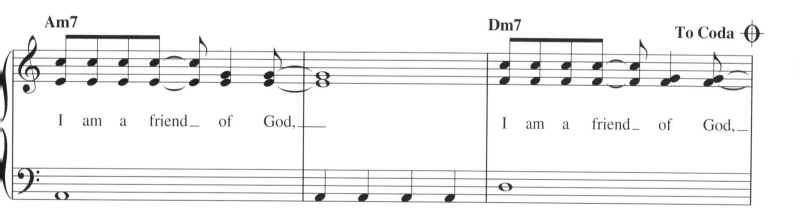

12

2. ___ He calls ___ me friend.

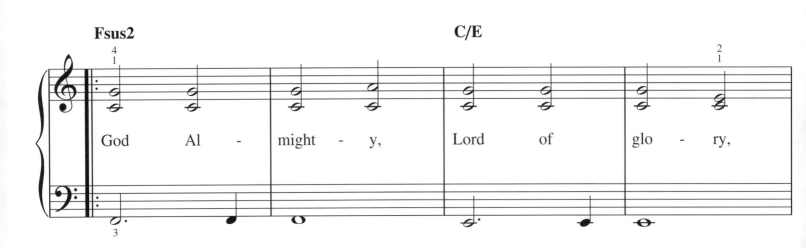
God Al - might - y, Lord of glo - ry,

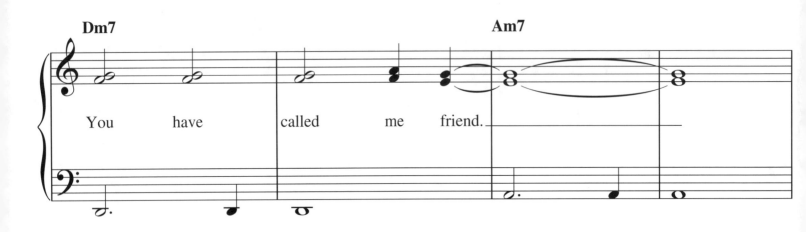
You have called me friend. ___

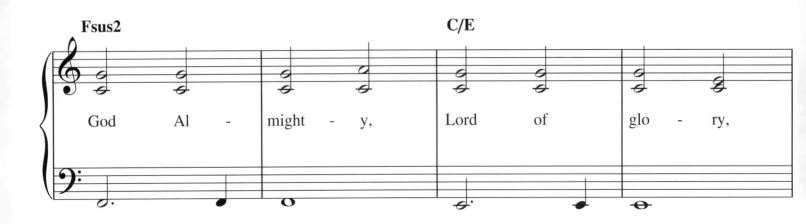
God Al - might - y, Lord of glo - ry,

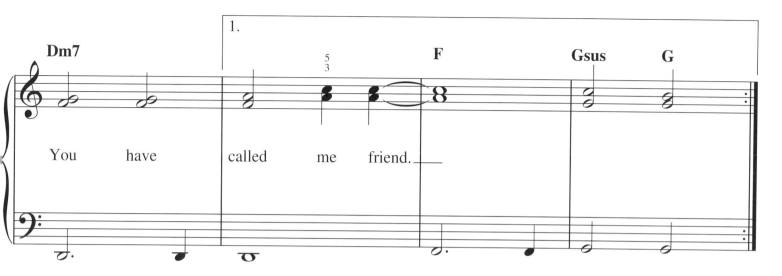
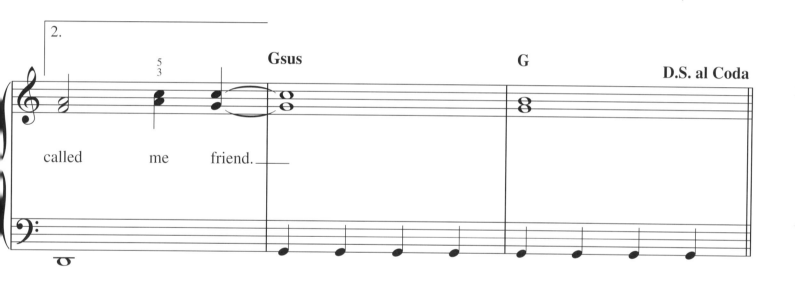
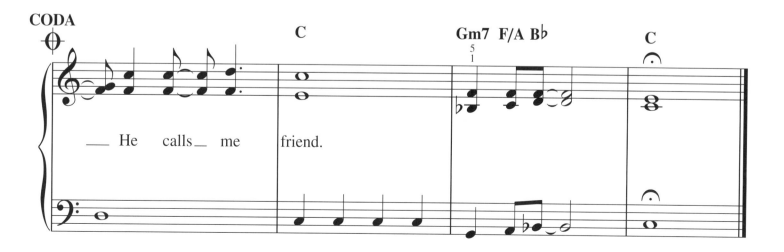

FREEDOM

Words and Music by
DARRELL EVANS

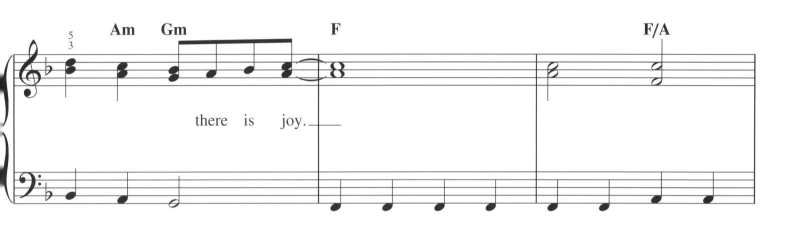
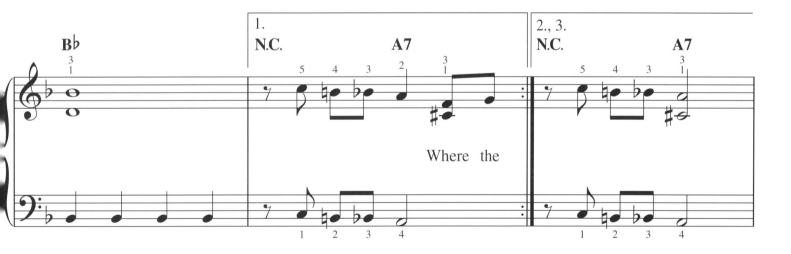

16

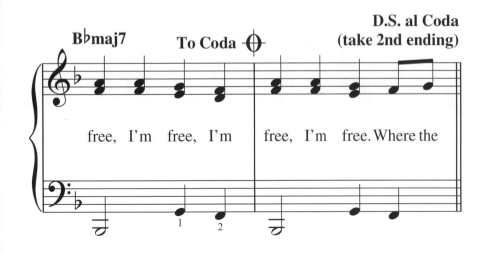

GOD IS GREAT

Words and Music by
MARTY SAMPSON

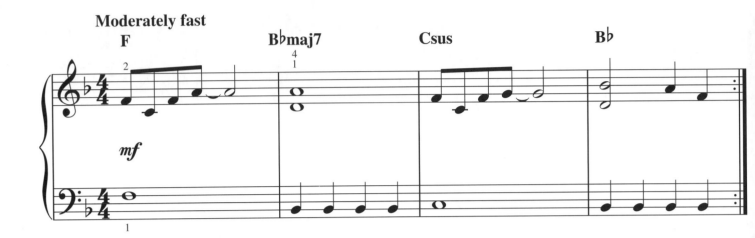

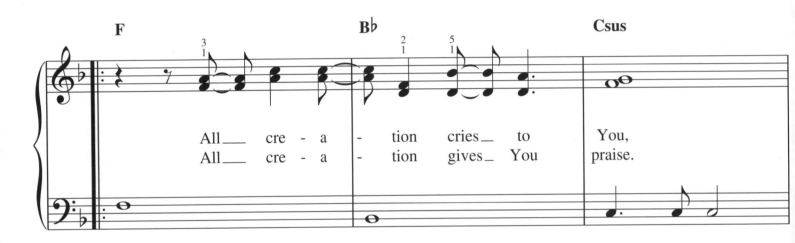

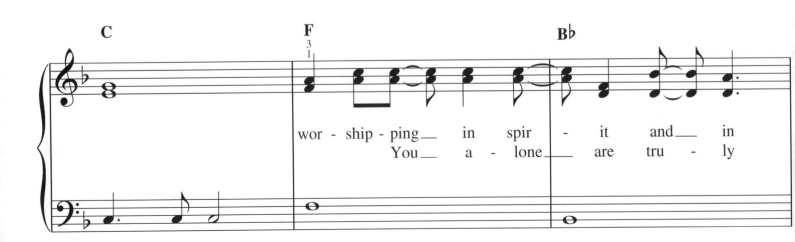

© 2001 Hillsong Publishing (admin. in the United States and Canada by Integrity's Hosanna! Music)/ASCAP
c/o Integrity Media, Inc., 1000 Cody Road, Mobile, AL 36695
All Rights Reserved   International Copyright Secured   Used by Permission

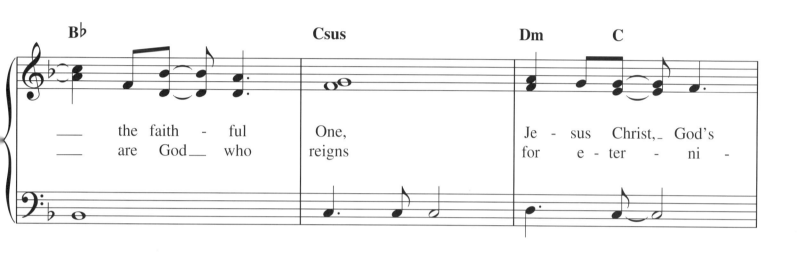

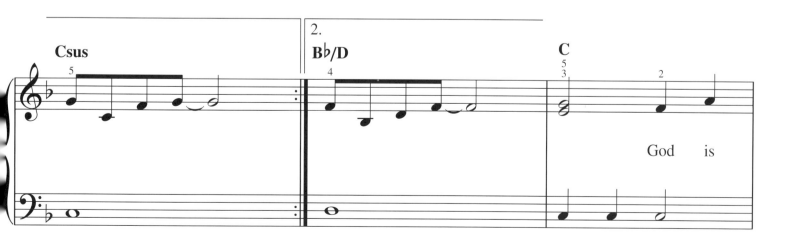

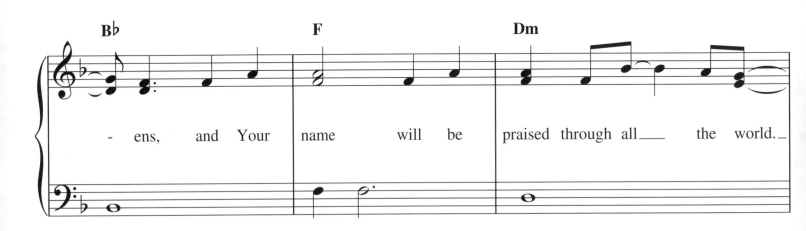

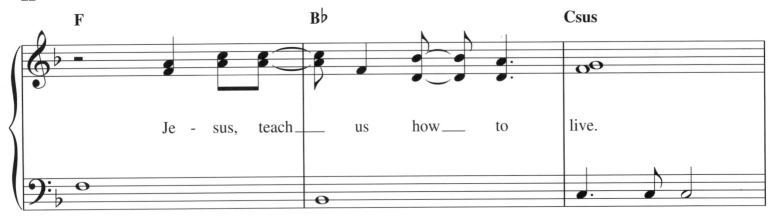

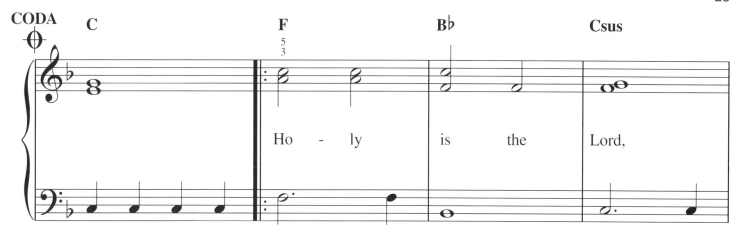
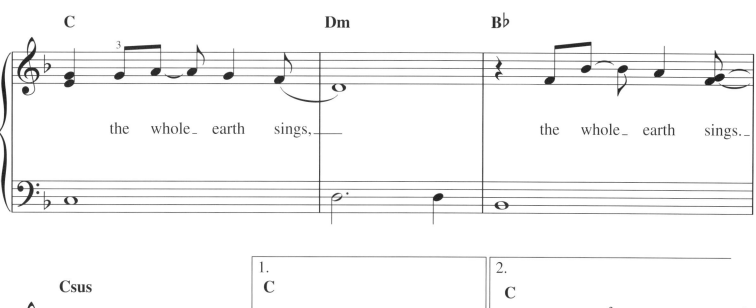

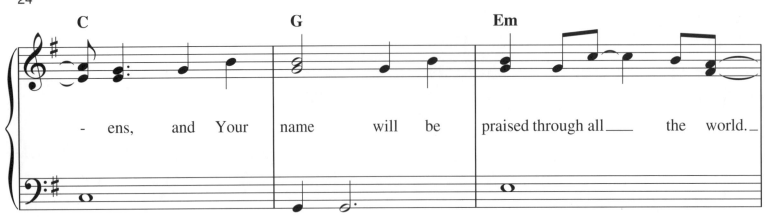

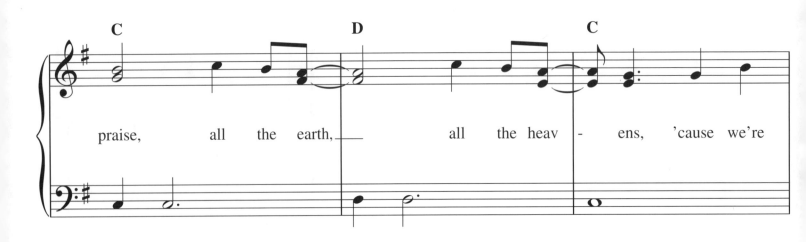

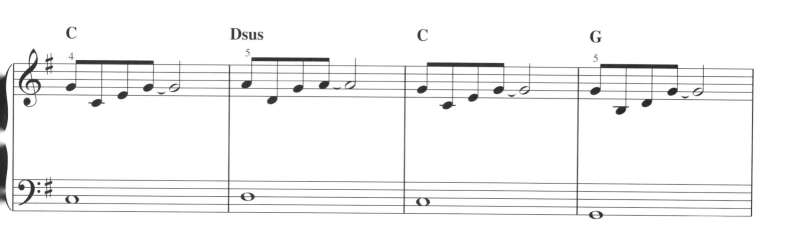

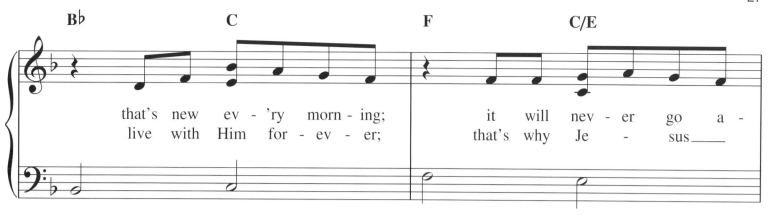

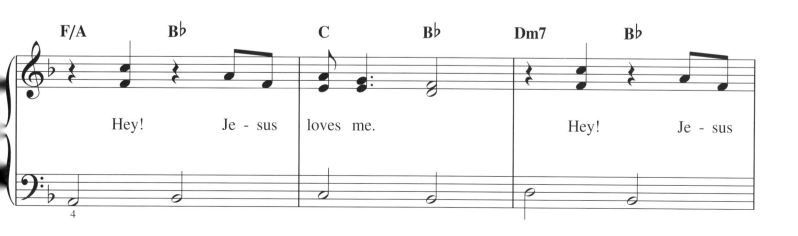

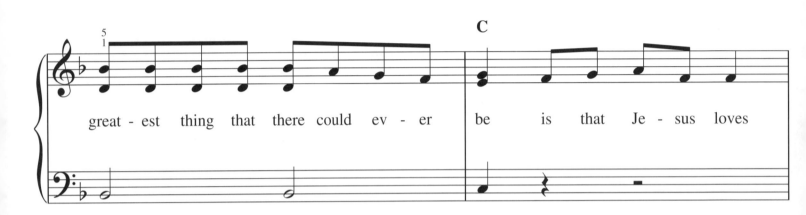
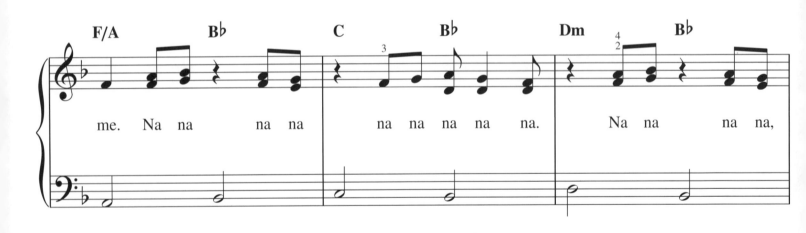
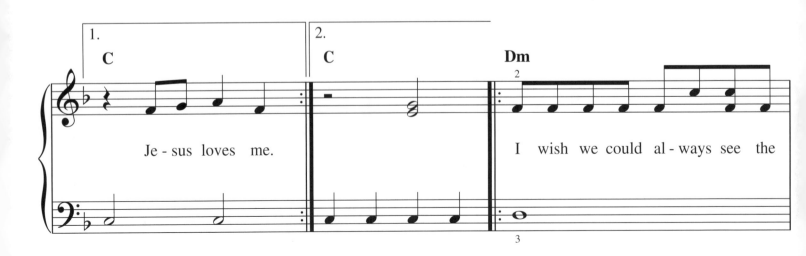

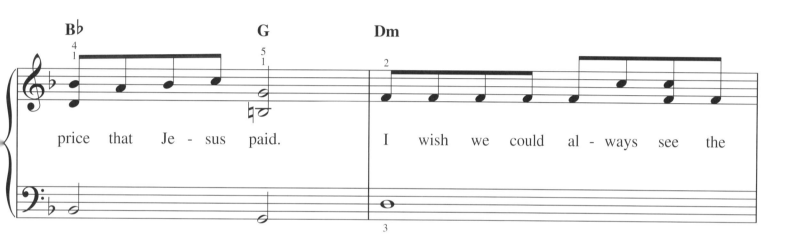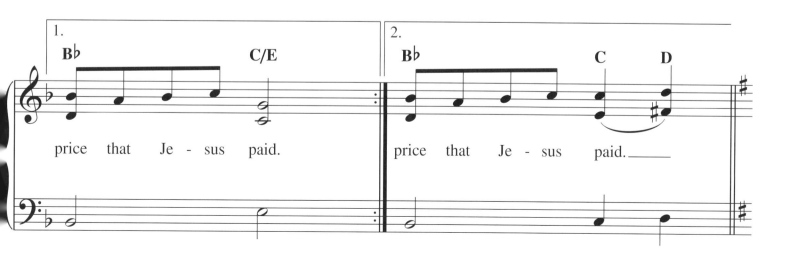

I GIVE YOU MY HEART

Words and Music by
REUBEN MORGAN

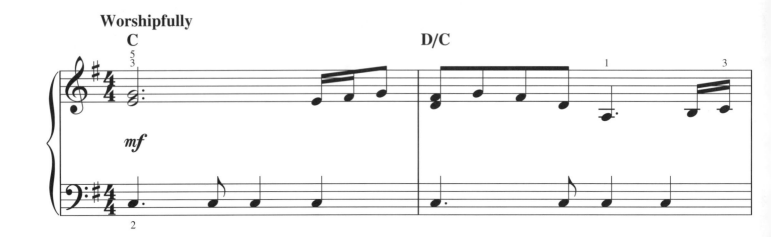
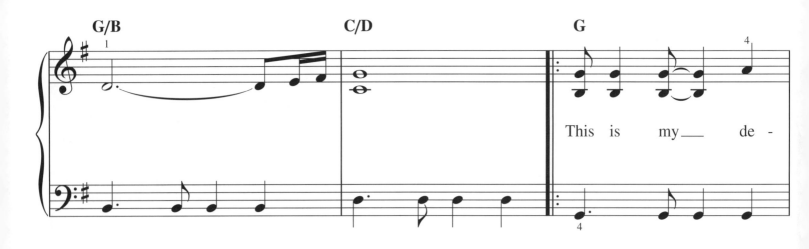
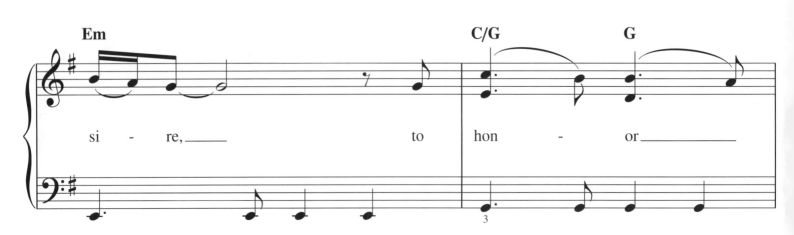

© 1995 Reuben Morgan and Hillsong Publishing (admin. in the U.S. and Canada by Integrity's Hosanna! Music)/ASCAP
c/o Integrity Media, Inc., 1000 Cody Road, Mobile, AL 36695
All Rights Reserved   International Copyright Secured   Used by Permission

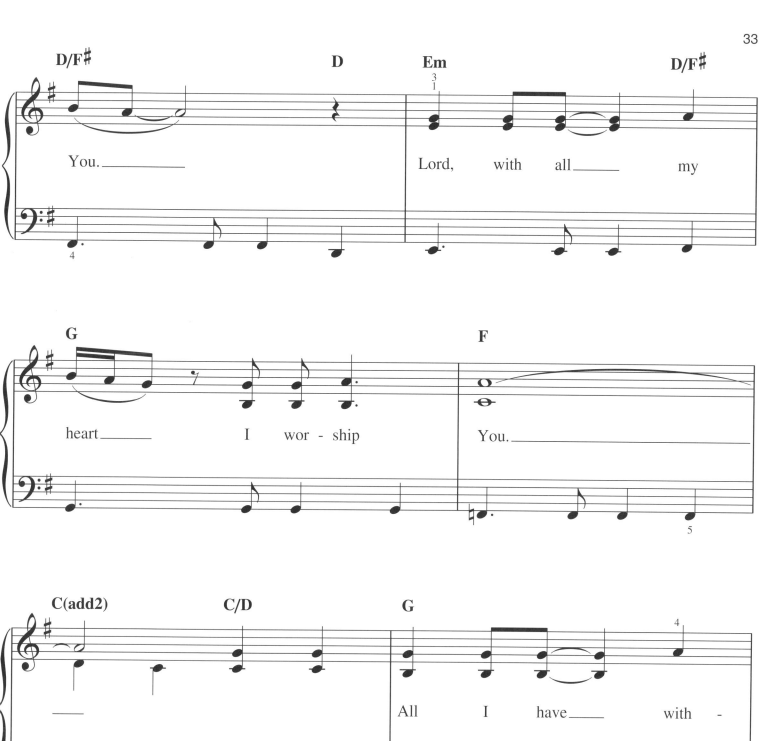

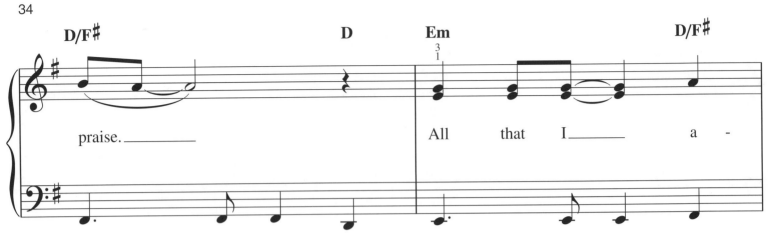
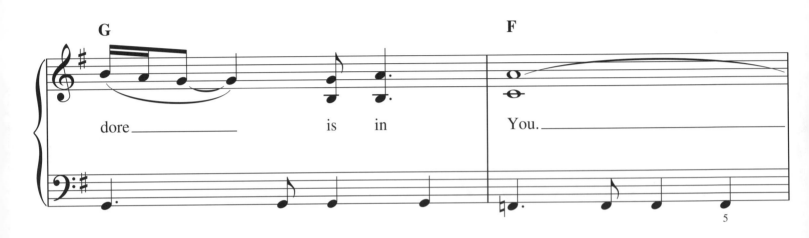
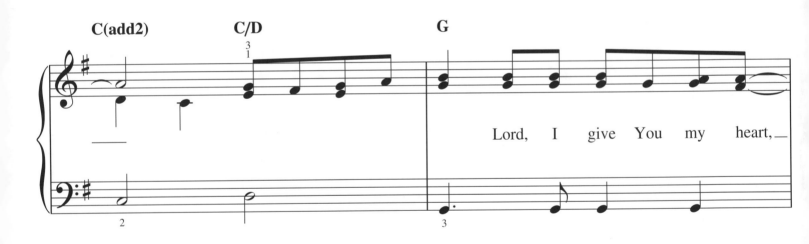

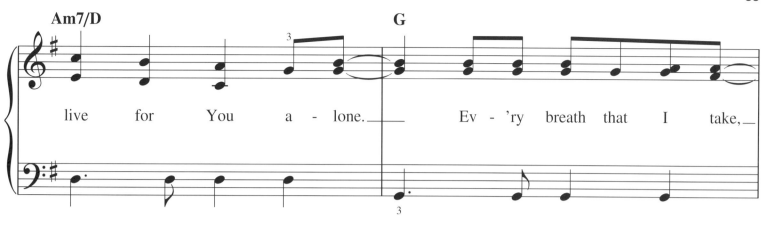

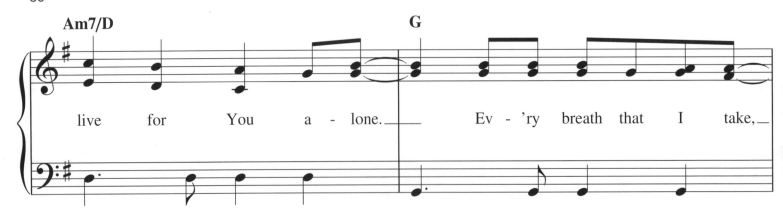
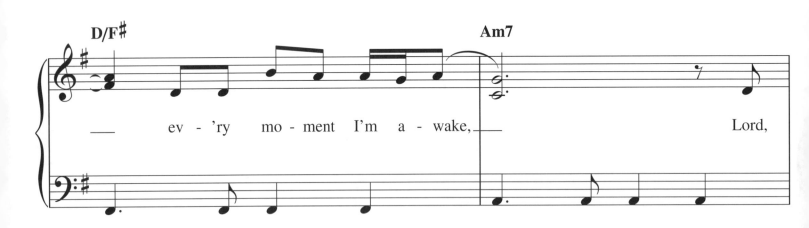
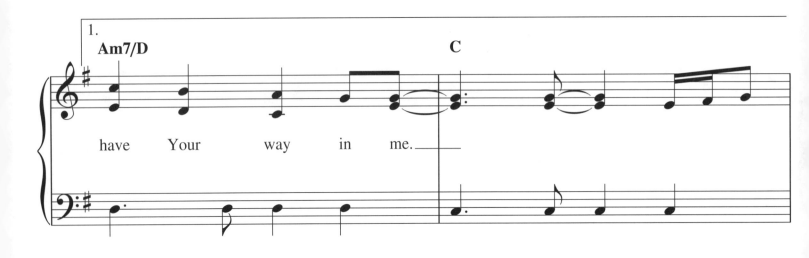
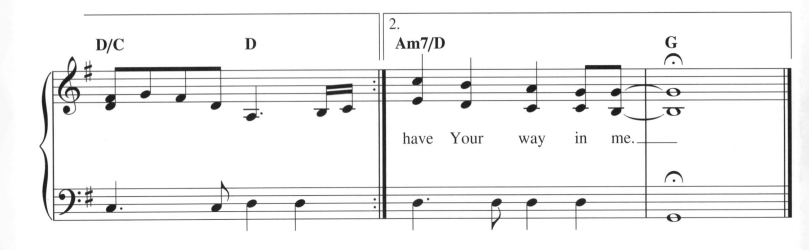

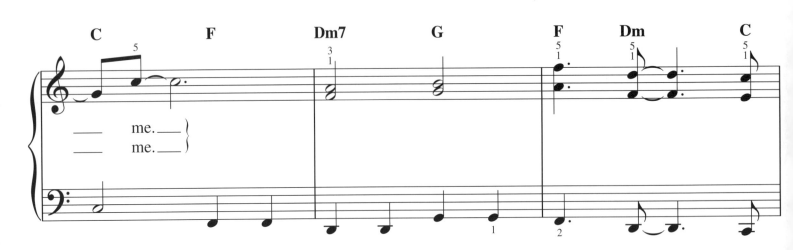

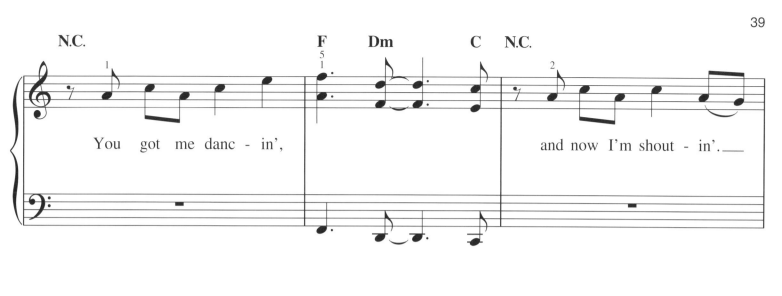

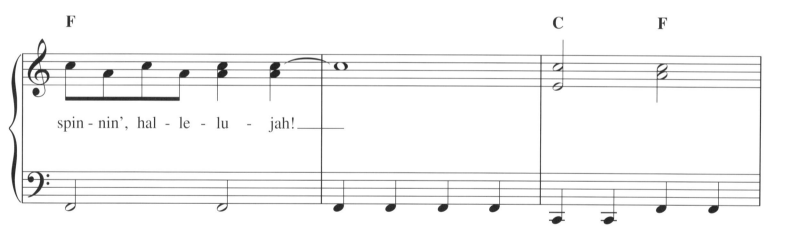
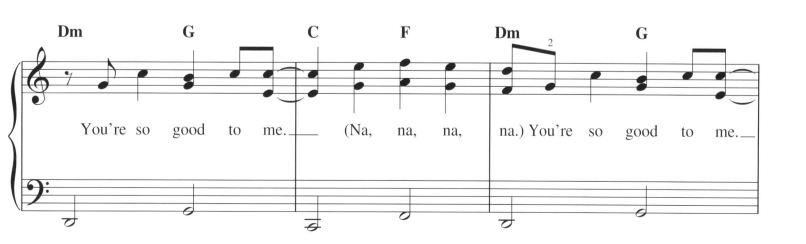

LET THE PRAISES RING

Words and Music by
LINCOLN BREWSTER

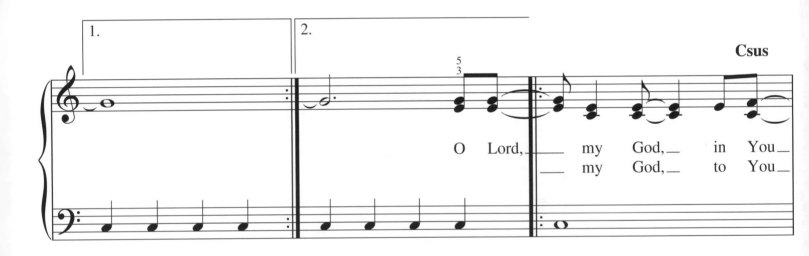

© 2002 Integrity's Praise! Music/BMI
c/o Integrity Media, Inc., 1000 Cody Road, Mobile, AL 36695
All Rights Reserved International Copyright Secured Used by Permission

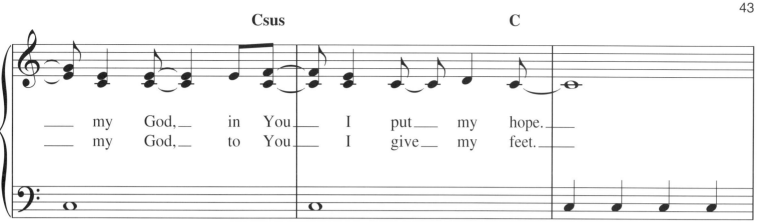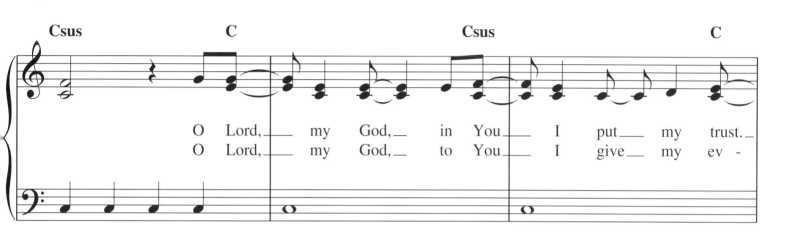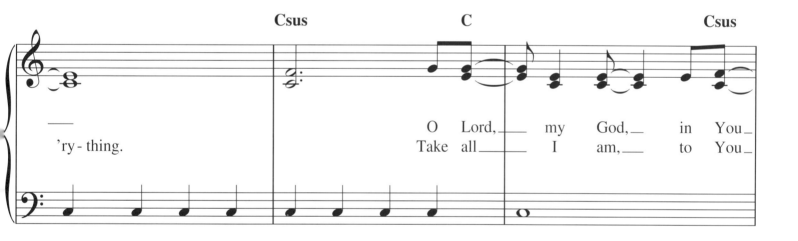

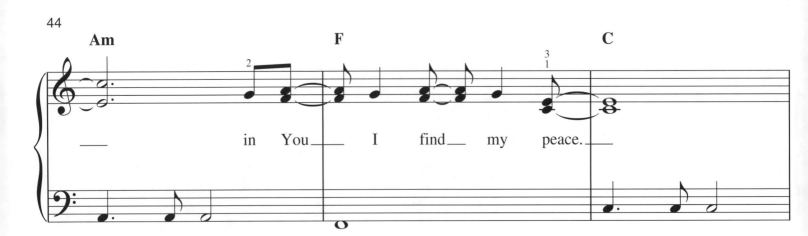

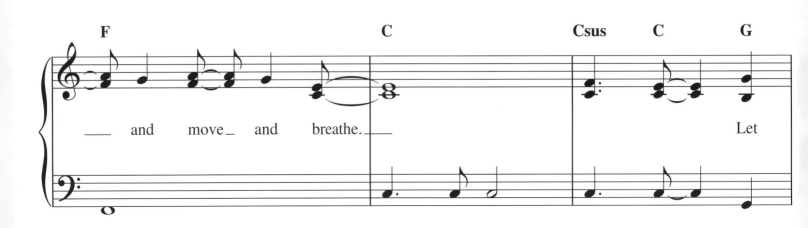

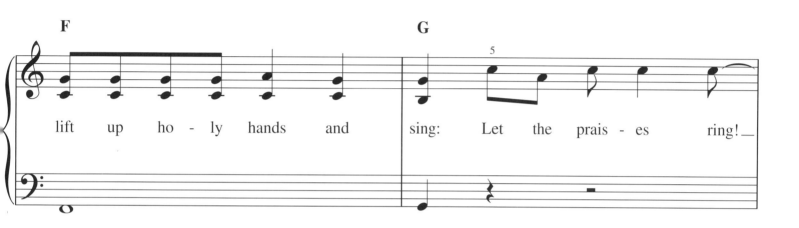

OPEN THE EYES OF MY HEART

Words and Music by
PAUL BALOCHE

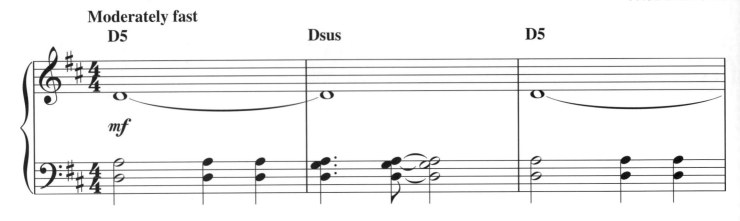
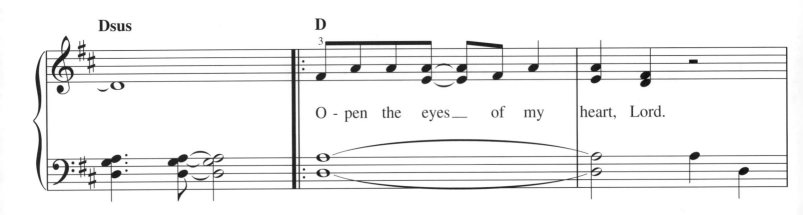

© 1997 Integrity's Hosanna! Music/ASCAP
c/o Integrity Media, Inc., 1000 Cody Road, Mobile, AL 36695
All Rights Reserved   International Copyright Secured   Used by Permission

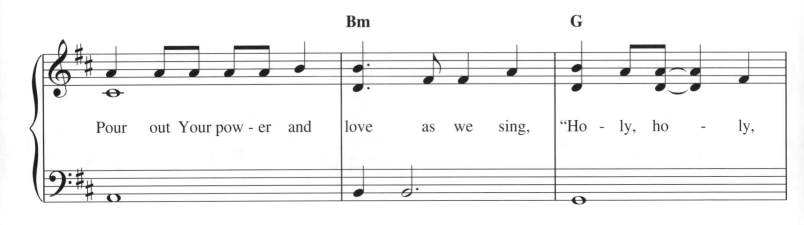
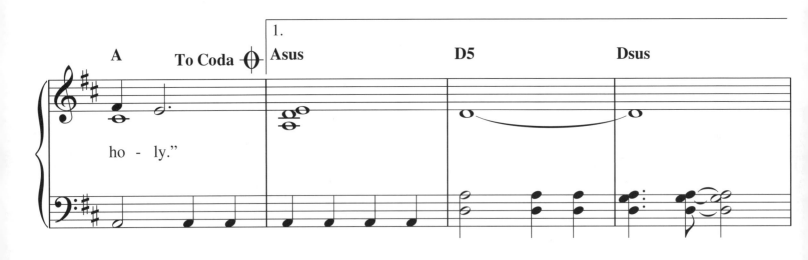
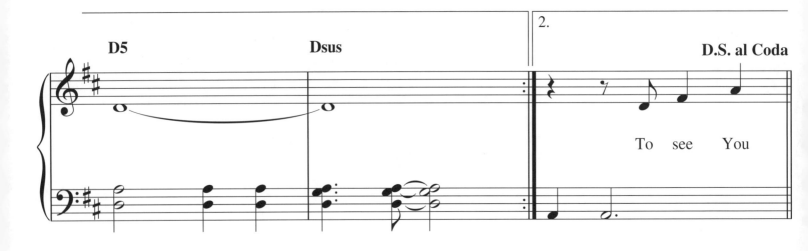
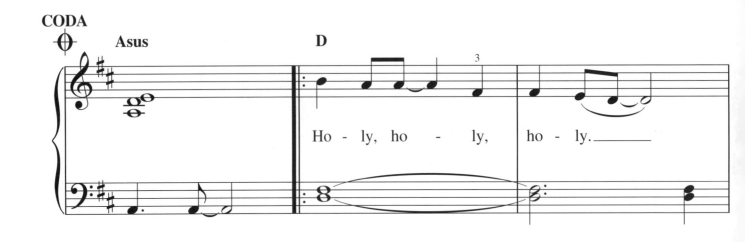

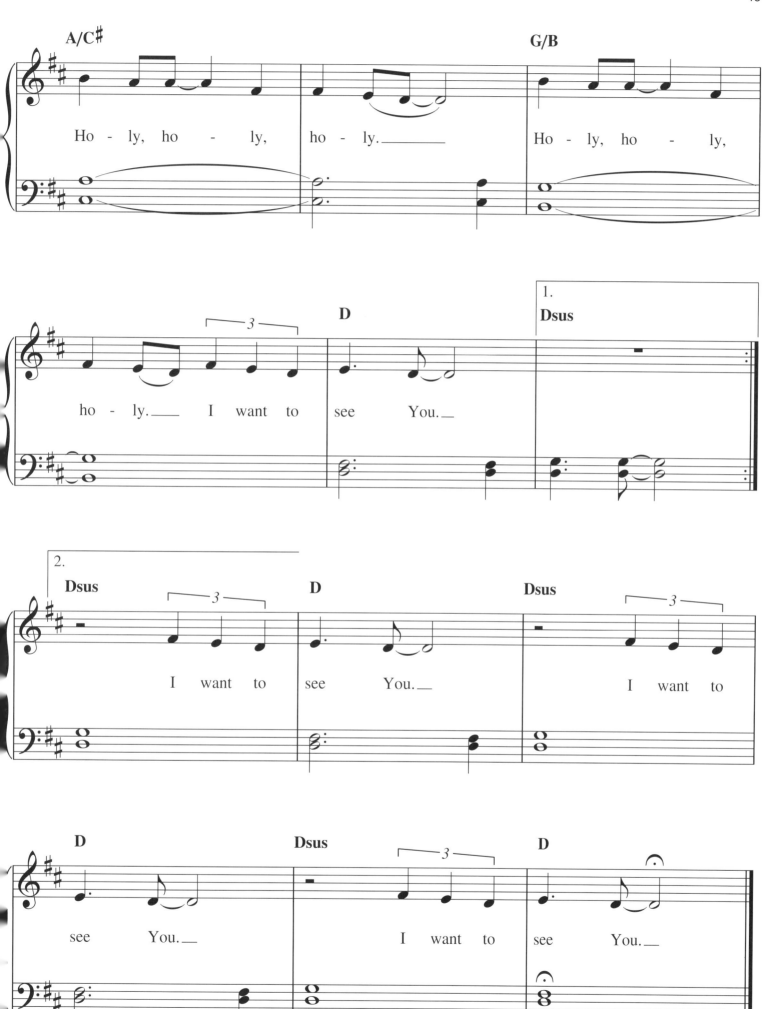

THANK YOU, LORD

Words and Music by PAUL BALOCHE
and DON MOEN

I come be-fore You to-day,_ and there's just one thing that I_
For all You've done in my life,_ You took my dark-ness and gave_

© 2004 Integrity's Hosanna! Music/ASCAP
c/o Integrity Media, Inc., 1000 Cody Road, Mobile, AL 36695
All Rights Reserved   International Copyright Secured   Used by Permission

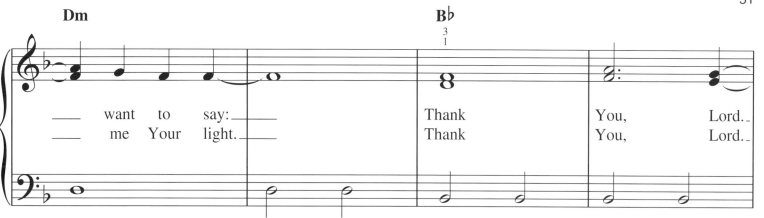
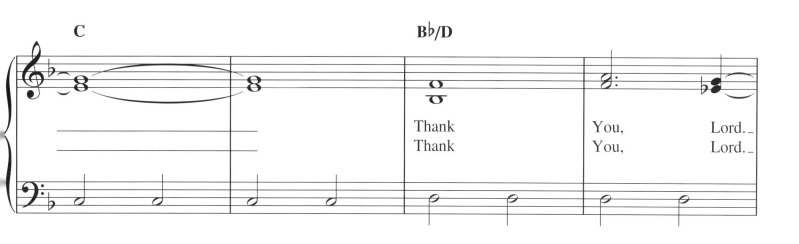
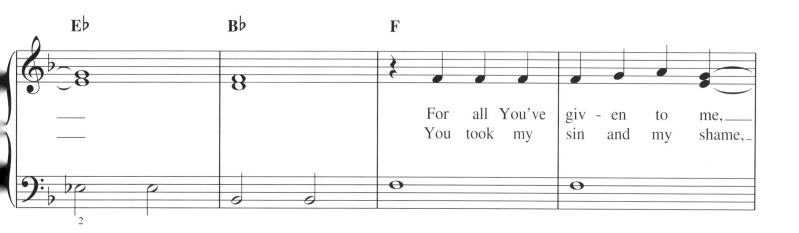
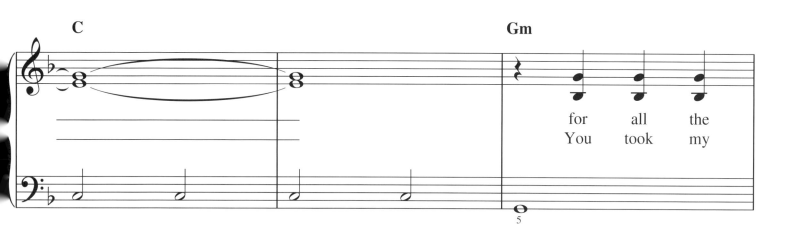

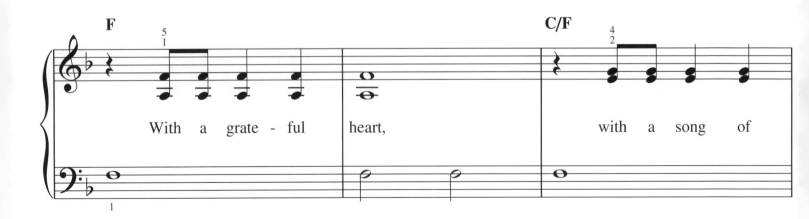

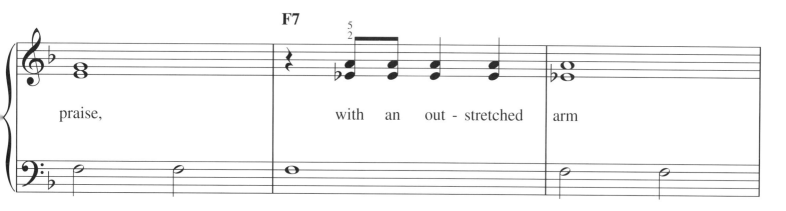
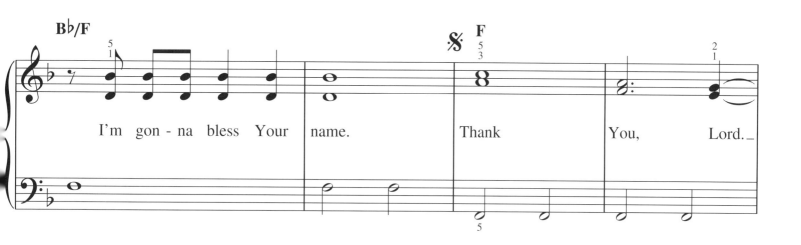

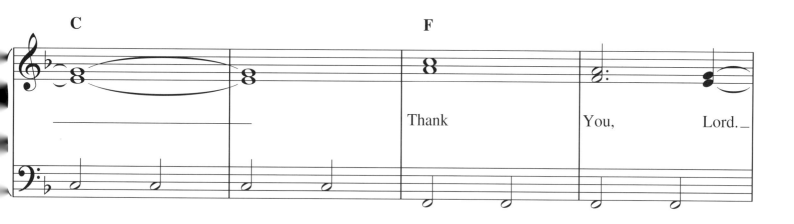

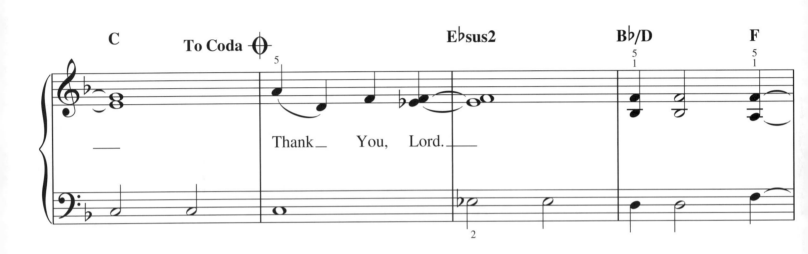
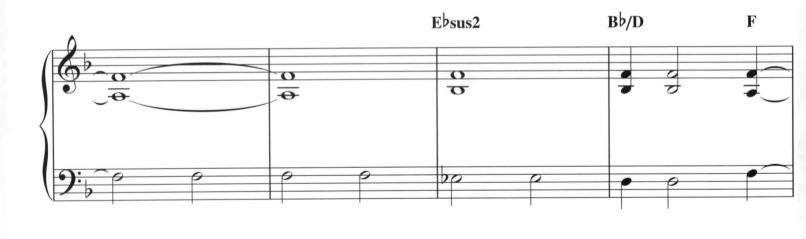
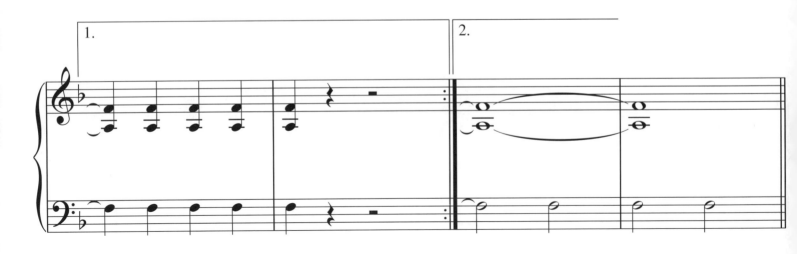

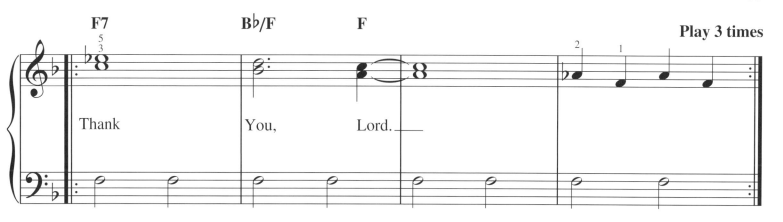
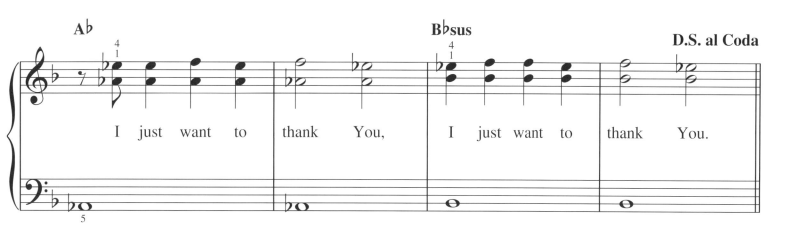
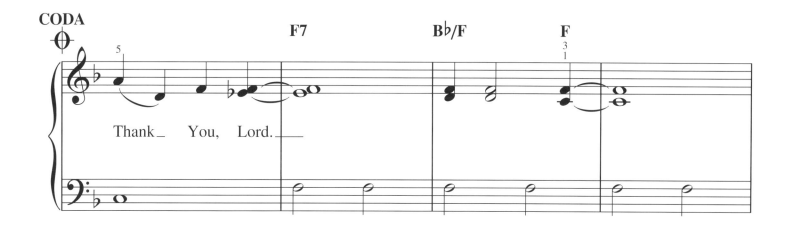
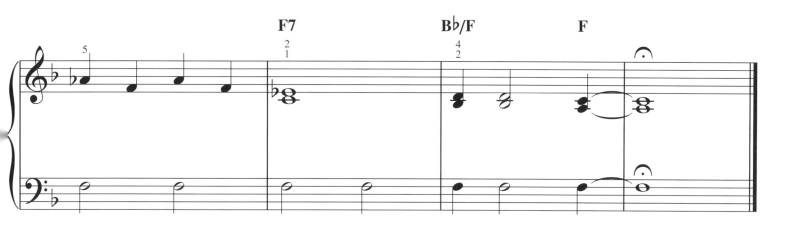

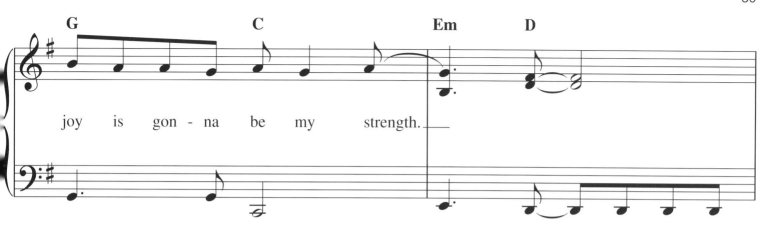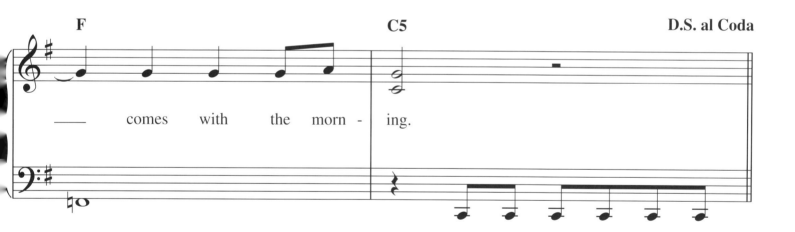

WE LIFT YOU UP

Words and Music by
GLENN PACKIAM

© 2002 Vertical Worship Songs/ASCAP
c/o Integrity Media, Inc., 1000 Cody Road, Mobile, AL 36695
All Rights Reserved International Copyright Secured Used by Permission

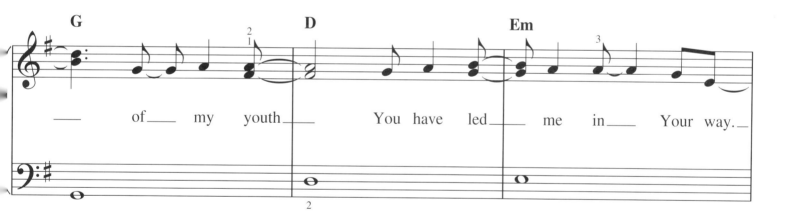
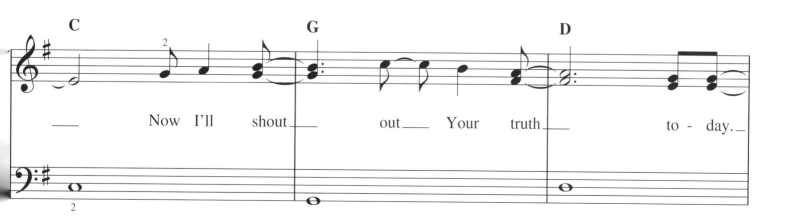

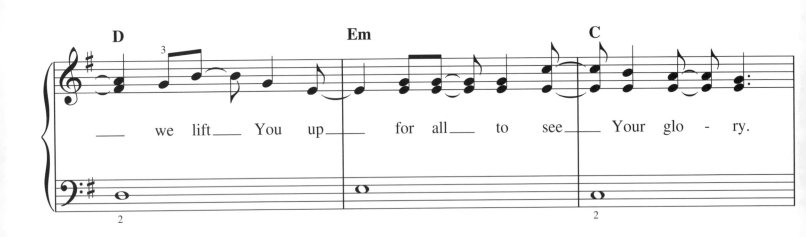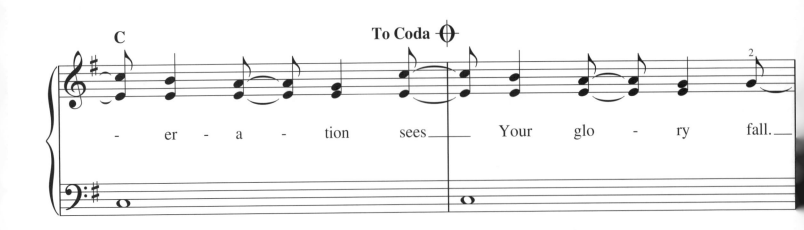

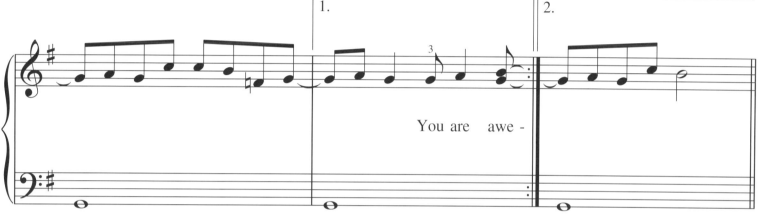

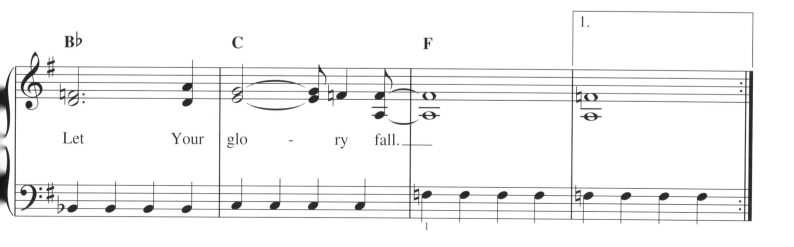